Paddington's Opposites

by Michael Bond

Illustrated by John Lobban
Devised by Carol Watson

PUFFIN BOOKS

Published by the Penguin Group
Penguin Books USA Inc., 375 Hudson Street, New York, New York 10014, U.S.A.
Penguin Books Canada Ltd, 10 Alcorn Avenue, Toronto, Ontario, Canada M4V 3B2

Penguin Books Ltd, Registered Offices: Harmondsworth, Middlesex, England

First published by William Collins Sons & Co. Ltd., 1990
First published in the United States of America by Viking,
a division of Penguin Books USA Inc., 1991
Published in Puffin Books, 1996

1 3 5 7 9 10 8 6 4 2

Text copyright © Michael Bond, 1990
Illustrations copyright © William Collins Sons & Co. Ltd., 1990
All rights reserved

Puffin Books ISBN 0-14-055765-2

Printed in Hong Kong

on

big

small

up

down

in

out

hot

cold

front

back

neat

messy

awake

asleep

wet

dry

open

closed

happy

sad

full

empty

clean

dirty

many

few

straight

crooked

Match the opposites.